Eskimos

Published in the United States by
Gloucester Press, in 1980

Originated and produced by
The Archon Press Ltd
70, Old Compton Street
London W1V 5PA

Designed by Louise Whale
Written by Jane Heath

First published in
Great Britain 1980 by
Hamish Hamilton Children's Books Ltd
Garden House, 57-59 Long Acre
London WC2

Printed in Great Britain by
W S Cowell Ltd
Butter Market, Ipswich

Certain illustrations originally published in
The Closer Look Series

Library of Congress
Catalog Card Number: 79-66170
ISBN 0-531-03418-6 (Lib. Bdg.)

Eskimos

Consultant editor
Henry Pluckrose

Illustrated by
Maurice Wilson

small world

Gloucester Press · New York · Toronto · 1980

Eskimos live in the Arctic where the weather is so cold that snow and ice cover the ground for much of the year. The winters are long and the summers are short. Even in summer the weather is cool. In the middle of winter there is no daylight at all; the sun never rises above the horizon.

Until about two hundred years ago, Eskimos lived undisturbed by the rest of the world. Up until then their way of life had not changed for hundreds of years. They were nomads; they had to keep moving around in search of food.
They lived in small groups with a few families in each group.

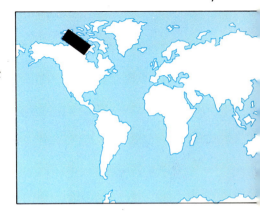

Coverings such as these
(above) were put over the
windows of stone igloos.

Because Eskimos lived a wandering life,
they did not have a permanent home. In
winter they built igloos of earth and
stone; in summer they lived in tents
made of animal skins.

The famous ice igloos were used by the men as shelter when they were away hunting. You crawl into an igloo through a tunnel. Inside it is warm; the heat comes from lamps which burn animal fat. The tunnel helps keep out the cold air.

The stone knife (above) was used to make the ice igloo.

Guillemot

Kittiwake

In the past Eskimos ate almost no vegetables or fruit. In the Arctic the weather is cold and the ground too hard for most plants to grow. In autumn there are a few berries. Most of the time Eskimos ate only meat. They caught most of their food in summer and stored it for the winter.

Walrus

Seal

Salmon

Cod

Narwhal

Whale

Char

In the sea Eskimos hunt seals, walrus, whales, narwhals and small fish. When birds fly north in summer Eskimos trap them and also collect their eggs. On land Eskimos shoot or trap big animals (like caribou and polar bears) and smaller ones (like foxes and rabbits).

Berries

Fox

Caribou

Polar Bear

Snow Goose

Ptarmigan

Eskimos used to cross snow and ice on sledges made of wood, bone or ivory. The sledges were pulled by dogs called huskies.

The number of huskies needed to pull a sledge varied with the size of the load and the length of the journey. Eskimos often made boots to protect the huskies' feet from the ice.

Eskimos built big boats, called umiaks, to
carry their families, dogs and belongings.
Umiaks were also used for hunting whales.

Kayaks are small boats
paddled by one man.
The frame is made of
wood or bone, and is
covered with sealskin.
They are used for hunting
at sea or on rivers.

084472

During the summer months Eskimos used to hunt whales. Here are some hunters setting out to catch whales using harpoons.

Sealskin bags full of air were tied to the tip of each harpoon. The floating bags tired the wounded whale as it dragged them through the water, while trying to escape.

Sealskin bags

Seals and walrus stay under the ice in winter.
They make breathing holes so they can come
up for air; this is when they can be caught.

Caribou are very important to Eskimos who
live inland. They eat caribou meat and use
the skins to make clothes and tents.

In spring herds of caribou migrate north.
The Eskimos shoot them on land or spear
them as they swim across lakes.

Many fish are caught,
dried and stored.

In summer Eskimos build dams to trap the
salmon and char that come up-river to breed.
The Eskimos stand in the water and stab the
fish with fish spears; then they thread
them on to lines held in their mouths.

Ulu

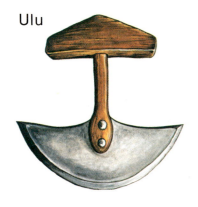

Eskimos used to depend on animals for almost everything they needed. The parts they did not eat were made into clothes and tools; nothing was wasted. Blubber, the fat of seals and whales, or caribou fat was used as fuel for lamps. Eskimos used their lamps for light, cooking, and even heating.

Here everyone is helping to cut up a whale and strip off its blubber.

Scrapers

Animal bones were used to build boats and sledges, and to make tools and harpoons. Women cut up skins with knives called ulus, to make clothes, tents, bags and boats. They sewed with thread made of sinew.

Before skins were used, the women scraped off the fat with special scrapers; then they washed and dried them and scraped them again. If the skins were tough, the women chewed them to make them soft.

If he was caught in a
snow storm, a hunter would
pull his arms inside his
parka and hold them
against his body for extra
warmth.
Eskimos wore two pairs
of boots. The inner
knee length boots or
socks were lined with
grass or moss.

Parka

Boots

In winter Eskimos have to keep warm in very, very cold temperatures, so they wear loose clothes made of caribou or sealskin. They wear two layers of skins, the inner layer with the fur turned inwards and the outer layer with the fur outwards. Many clothes have beautiful patterns on them.

Snow goggles protected their eyes from the glare off the snow.

A woman wearing sealskin clothes.

Here is another style of seal-skin clothing.

This jacket is made of eider duck skins.

Finger pulling is
a popular game among
Eskimo men and boys.

This woman is trying
to catch a piece of
pierced bone on a pin.

In this game, called
nuglutang, children
try to spear a bit of
ivory with a hole in it.

Autumn was the Eskimos' time for feasting;
they danced, sang and chanted poetry.
Their songs and dances told a story — perhaps
about hunting or the coming of summer.
They enjoyed games of strength, like weight-
lifting and wrestling, and they also played
board games. Nowadays they also play football.

These people are playing
the game skin toss. One
Eskimo at a time jumps
up and down on a walrus
skin held tight by people
standing round in a circle.
The one who jumps the
highest wins the game.

Eskimos carve beautiful figures out of bone, wood, antler and ivory from walrus tusks. They carve dolls, games for the children and animal figures. They used to think the animal figures were lucky charms, which gave people special skills and brought good hunting and protection from evil spirits.

Eskimos used to carve with bow drills; now they use modern tools. Here an old man is using a bow drill. He would have carved such things as the objects above, the wooden doll and bird, and the lucky animal charms.

Besides carving figures, the
Eskimos also painted pictures which
recorded every day events like the
hunt or their feasts and celebrations.

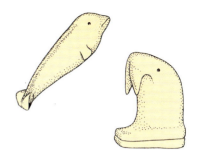

Below is an Eskimo
drawing of the men in
the dance house. They
danced to the beat of
the tambourine-like
drums that you can see in the
the drawing. Often in their
dances they would wear
strange wooden masks
like this one.

But the life of the Eskimo has changed.
Snowmobiles, like the one in the picture,
have replaced dog sledges. Children go to
school and learn new and different skills.
Life is more comfortable but the old skills
and culture of the Eskimo are in danger of
disappearing for ever.

Index